Benjamin H. Brewster

The new public buildings on Penn Square, in the city of Philadelphia:

Address of Hon. Benjamin Harris Brewster, at the laying of the corner stone, July 4, 1874, with a description of the buildings, the statistics and progress of the work up to Janua

Benjamin H. Brewster

The new public buildings on Penn Square, in the city of Philadelphia:
Address of Hon. Benjamin Harris Brewster, at the laying of the corner stone, July 4, 1874, with a description of the buildings, the statistics and progress of the work up to Janua

ISBN/EAN: 9783337713430

Printed in Europe, USA, Canada, Australia, Japan

Cover: Foto ©ninafisch / pixelio.de

More available books at **www.hansebooks.com**

THE

𝔑𝔢𝔴 𝔓𝔲𝔟𝔩𝔦𝔠 𝔅𝔲𝔦𝔩𝔡𝔦𝔫𝔤𝔰,

ON

PENN SQUARE,

IN THE CITY OF PHILADELPHIA.

ADDRESS OF HON. BENJAMIN HARRIS BREWSTER, AT THE
LAYING OF THE CORNER STONE, JULY 4, 1874;

WITH A DESCRIPTION OF THE BUILDINGS,

THE STATISTICS AND PROGRESS OF THE WORK UP TO
JANUARY 1, 1880,

AND A SUMMARY OF LEGISLATIVE AND MUNICIPAL
ACTION RELATING TO THE UNDERTAKING;

WITH A BRIEF HISTORY OF EVENTS PERTAINING
THERETO.

PRINTED FOR THE COMMISSIONERS.

PHILADELPHIA:
1880.

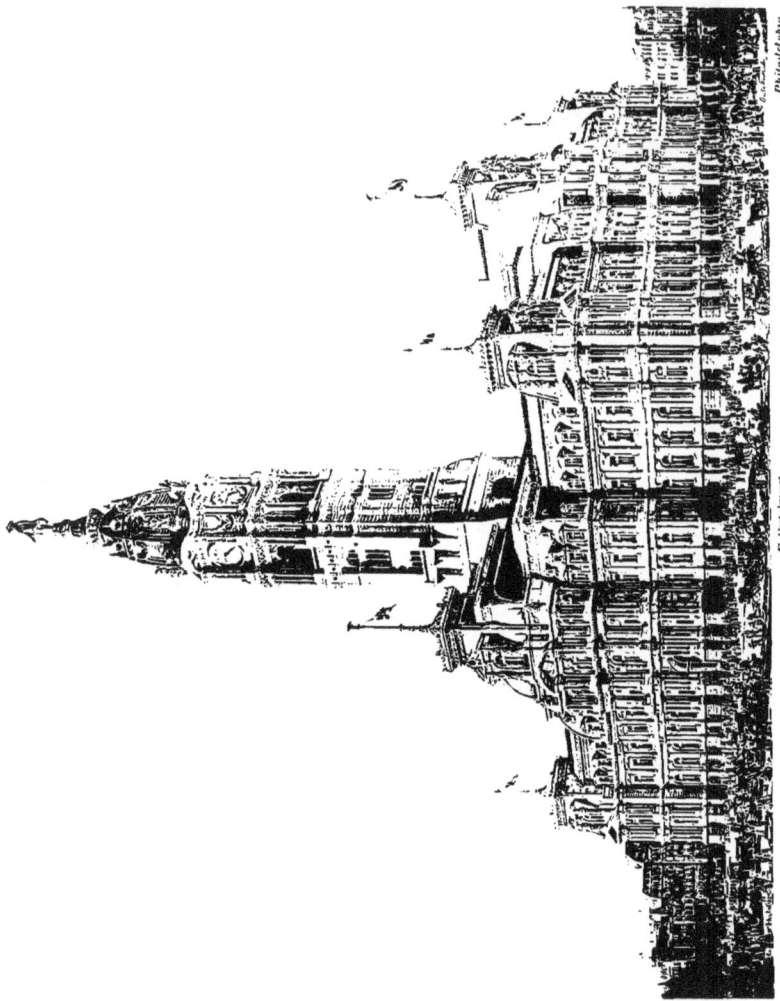

Phototype.

F. Gutekunst.

Philadelphia

NEW PUBLIC BUILDINGS, PENN SQUARE, PHILADELPHIA, PA.

John McArthur, Jr., Architect.

THE

𝕹𝖊𝖜 𝕻𝖚𝖇𝖑𝖎𝖈 𝕭𝖚𝖎𝖑𝖉𝖎𝖓𝖌𝖘,

ON

PENN SQUARE,

IN THE CITY OF PHILADELPHIA.

———

ADDRESS OF HON. BENJAMIN HARRIS BREWSTER, AT THE
LAYING OF THE CORNER STONE, JULY 4, 1874;

WITH A DESCRIPTION OF THE BUILDINGS,

THE STATISTICS AND PROGRESS OF THE WORK UP TO
JANUARY 1, 1880,

AND A SUMMARY OF LEGISLATIVE AND MUNICIPAL
ACTION RELATING TO THE UNDERTAKING;

WITH A BRIEF HISTORY OF EVENTS PERTAINING
THERETO.

-

PRINTED FOR THE COMMISSIONERS.

-

PHILADELPHIA:
1880.

PRESS OF HENRY B. ASHMEAD,

1102 AND 1104 SANSOM STREET, PHILADELPHIA.

COMMISSIONERS

For the Erection of the Public Buildings.

THOMAS J. BARGER,
WILLIAM BRICE,
ISAAC S. CASSIN,
JOSEPH L. CAVEN,
SAMUEL W. CATTELL,
MAHLON H. DICKINSON,

THOMAS E. GASKILL,
JOHN L. HILL,
HIRAM MILLER,
RICHARD PELTZ,
SAMUEL C. PERKINS,
GEORGE A. SMITH,

WILLIAM S. STOKLEY.

OFFICERS.

President.

SAMUEL C. PERKINS.

Secretary.

FRANCIS DE HAES JANVIER.

Treasurer.

J. J. MARTIN.

Solicitor.

CHARLES H. T. COLLIS.

Architect.

JOHN McARTHUR, Jr.

Assistants.

JOHN ORD, Jr.   THOMAS U. WALTER.

Superintendent.

WILLIAM C. McPHERSON.

The bill providing for the erection of New Public Buildings for the City of Philadelphia passed both branches of the State Legislature in April, 1870, and on the 5th of the following August, the Governor affixed his signature thereto.

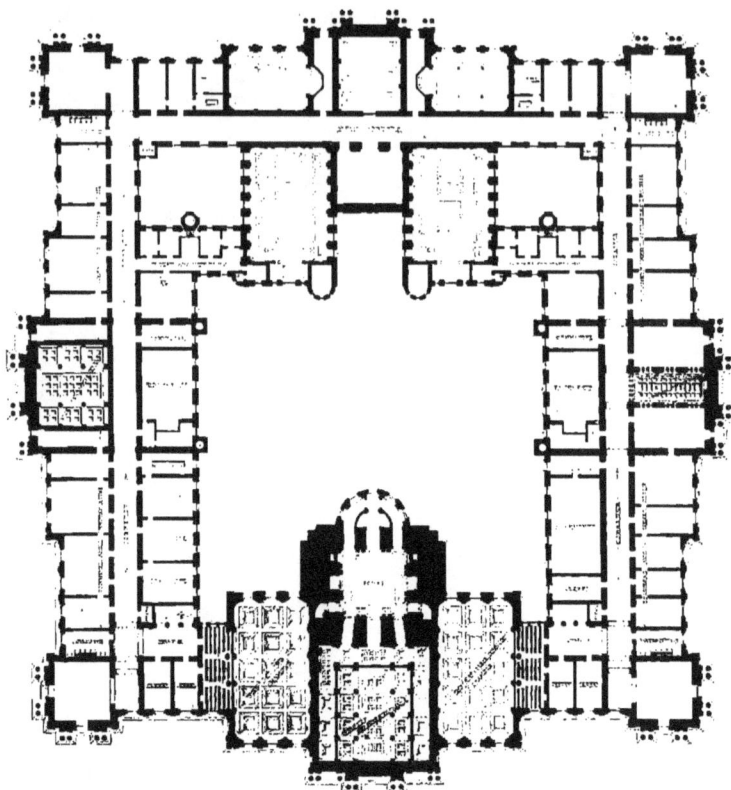

NORTH.

SCALE   60 FEET.

PRINCIPAL FLOOR—NEW PUBLIC BUILDINGS—PHILADELPHIA.

John McArthur, Jr. Architect.

Phototype.   *F. Gutekunst.*   *Philadelphia.*

AN ACT

Erection of the Public Buildings.

An Act *to provide for the erection of all the Public Buildings required to accommodate the Courts, and for all Municipal purposes, in the City of Philadelphia, and to require the appropriation, by said City, of Penn Squares, at Broad and Market Streets, to the Academy of Fine Arts, the Academy of Natural Sciences, the Franklin Institute, and the Philadelphia Library, in the event of the said Squares not being selected by a vote of the people as the site for the Public Buildings for said City.*

Section 1. BE IT ENACTED by the Senate and House of Representatives of the Commonwealth of Pennsylvania, in General Assembly met, and it is hereby enacted by the authority of the same : That THEODORE CUYLER, JOHN RICE, SAMUEL C. PERKINS, JOHN PRICE WETHERILL, LEWIS C. CASSIDY, HENRY M. PHILLIPS, WILLIAM L. STOKES, WILLIAM DEVINE, the MAYOR OF THE CITY OF PHILADELPHIA, and the PRESIDENTS OF SELECT AND COMMON COUNCILS, for the time being, are constituted Commissioners for the erection of the Public Buildings required to accommodate the Courts, and for all Municipal purposes, in the City of Philadelphia, who shall organize within thirty days, procure such plans for the said buildings adapted to either of said sites hereinafter named, as in their judgment may be needful ; appoint of their own number, a President, and from other than their own number, a Secretary, Treasurer, Solicitor, a competent Architect and assistants, and other employees ; fix the compensation of each person employed by them, and do all other acts necessary in their judgment to carry out the intent of this act in relation to said Public Buildings; fill any vacancies which may happen by death, resignation, or otherwise ; and if in the judgment of said Commission, they shall deem it advisable to increase their number, they may, by a vote of a majority of their whole number, increase said Commission from time to time to any number not exceeding thirteen. The said Commissioners are hereby authorized and directed to locate said buildings on either Washington Square or Penn Square, as may be determined by a vote of the legally qualified voters of the City of Philadelphia, at the next general election in October, one thousand eight hundred and seventy, and the Sheriff shall issue his proclamation, and the City Commissioners and other proper officers of said City shall provide all things that may be needful to enable the voters to decide by ballot their choice of a site for said Public Buildings, and the Return Clerks shall certify to the Prothonotary the result of said election in the usual form required for other elections. And as soon as said choice is determined by a vote of the people, as provided in this act, the said Commissioners shall, within thirty days thereafter, advertise for proposals, and make all needful contracts for the construction of said buildings, as soon thereafter as may be found practicable, which contracts shall be valid and binding in law upon the City, and upon the Contractors, when approved by a majority of the said Board of Commissioners ; and the said Commissioners shall make requisition on the Councils of said City, prior to the first day of December in each year, for the amount of money required by them for the purposes of the Commission for the succeeding year, and said Councils shall levy a special tax, sufficient to raise the amount so required : *Provided*, That said Councils may at any time make appropriations out of the annual tax in aid of the purposes of this act. *And provided further*, That the amount to be expended by said Commissioners shall be strictly limited to the sum required to satisfy their contracts for the erection of said buildings, and for the proper and complete furnishing thereof; and as soon as any part of said buildings may be completed and furnished ready for occupancy, they shall be occupied by the Courts, or such branch of the Municipal Government as they are in-

tended for by said Commissioners; and upon the completion of a sufficient portion of said buildings to accommodate the Courts and Municipal
Offices, the buildings now occupied by them respectively shall be vacated
and removed, and upon the entire completion of the new buildings, all
the present buildings on Independence Square, except Independence
Hall, shall be removed, and the ground placed in good condition by said
Commission as part of their duty under this act, the expense of which
shall be paid out of their general fund provided by this act, and there-
upon the said Independence Square shall be and remain a public walk
and green for ever.

And be it further provided, That in the event of Washington Square
being selected by a majority of votes as the location for the said Public
Buildings, then and in that event, the Councils of the City of Philadelphia are hereby authorized, empowered, and required to set apart for and
convey by proper deeds or grants of conveyance, or by proper assurances
of the right to occupy said squares, which the Mayor of Philadelphia
shall duly sign and execute under the seal of said City, the four squares
of ground, known as Penn Squares, located at the intersection of Broad
and Market Streets, in the City of Philadelphia, as laid down on the
present map of said City, one to each of the following institutions: the
Academy of Fine Arts, the Academy of Natural Sciences, the Franklin
Institute, and the Philadelphia Library, for the purpose of allowing them
to erect thereon ornamental and suitable buildings for their respective
institutions. The location of such buildings and the plans thereof to be
approved by the Commissioners appointed under this act, and their suc-
cessors in office, together with the time of erection, and all other matters
appertaining thereto: *Provided, however*, That all expenses connected
with said conveyances, plans, and other information requisite for the said
Commission to have, shall be paid by the institutions respectively. In
the event of the ultimate selection of Penn Squares as the site for said
Public Buildings, the said Commission shall have authority and they are
hereby empowered to vacate so much of Market and Broad Streets
as they may deem needful: *Provided, however*, That the streets passing
around said buildings shall not be of less width than one hundred feet.

It shall be the duty of the Mayor, the City Controller, City Commissioners, and City Treasurer, and of all other officers of the City, and also the duty of the Councils of the City of Philadelphia, to do and perform all such acts, in aid and promotion of the intent and purpose of this Act of Assembly, as said Commission may from time to time require. All laws and parts of laws restricting the uses and purposes of said Squares, or any of them, that may be in conflict with the intention and purpose of this act, be and the same are hereby repealed.

B. B. STRANG,
Speaker of the House of Representatives.

CHARLES H. STINSON,
Speaker of the Senate.

Approved the fifth day of August, Anno Domini one thousand eight hundred and seventy.

JOHN W. GEARY.

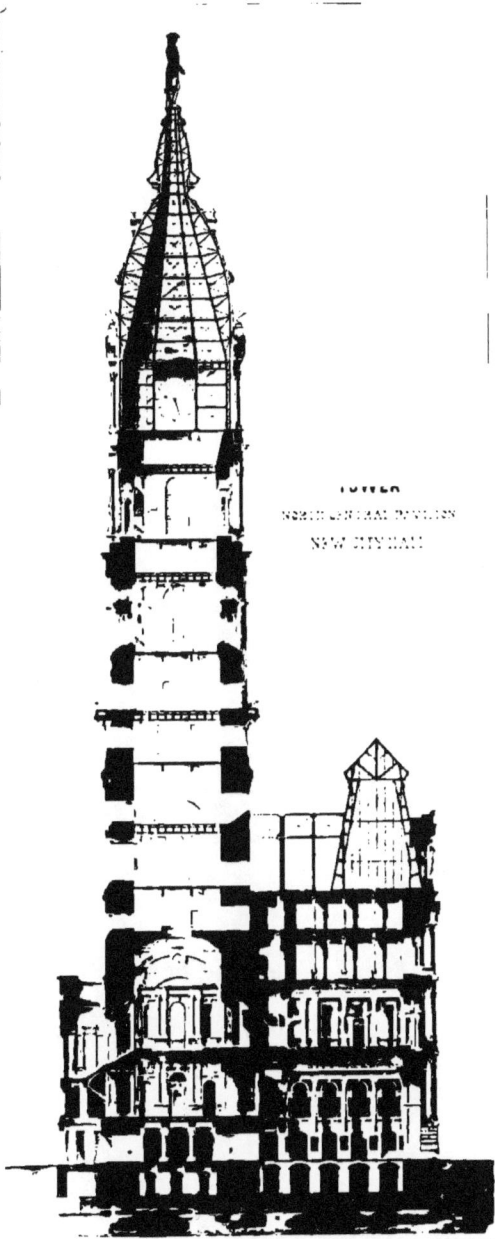

TOWER
NORTH CENTRAL PAVILION
NEW CITY HALL

THE corner stone was laid July 4, 1874, by ALFRED R. POTTER, Esq., R. W. Grand Master of Masons of Pennsylvania, in compliance with a request made by a Committee of the Commissioners, appointed in pursuance of a resolution unanimously adopted June 2, 1874. At this time the larger portion of the excavations had been completed and the foundations were in a good state of forwardness.

The Hon. WILLIAM S. STOKLEY, Mayor of the City and *ex officio* a member of the Public Building Commission, acted as President of the day.

The R. W. Grand Master was assisted by the elected and appointed Grand Officers of the " R. W. Grand Lodge of F. & A. M. of Pennsylvania and Masonic Jurisdiction thereunto belonging," and attended by a large number of the brethren.

The corner stone was laid in the northeast angle of the tower foundations, and was of a block of fine white marble, weighing about eight tons, from the quarries at Lee, Massachusetts, which have furnished the material for the facing of the entire superstructure above the basement. Upon the upper side of the stone a cavity was made in which was placed an hermetically sealed copper box, in which were deposited coins, documents, newspapers of the day, &c., &c.

One face of the stone is exposed to view from the interior

space in the centre of the tower foundation, and upon this face is cut the following inscription :—

CORNER STONE

OF THE

PUBLIC BUILDINGS OF THE CITY OF PHILADELPHIA,

LAID JULY 4, 1874,

In the presence of the Mayor of the City, the Select and Common Councils, Heads of Departments, and other distinguished Civil, Military, and Naval Officials, and a large concourse of citizens,

By ALFRED R. POTTER, Esq.,

R. W. Grand Master of Masons of Pennsylvania and Masonic Jurisdiction thereunto belonging, assisted by his Grand Officers, and according to the ancient ceremonies of the craft.

Orator—BENJAMIN HARRIS BREWSTER.

President of the United States.	Governor of Pennsylvania.	Mayor of Philadelphia.
ULYSSES S. GRANT,	JOHN F. HARTRANFT,	WILLIAM S. STOKLEY.

Architect—JOHN McARTHUR, JR.   Superintendent—WILLIAM C. McPHERSON.

Commissioners for the Erection of the Public Buildings.

Act of Assembly, August 5, 1870.

PRESIDENT—SAMUEL C. PERKINS.

Thos. J. Barger,	Lewis C. Cassidy,	Thomas E. Gaskill,	Hiram Miller,
William Brice,	Mahlon H. Dickinson,	A. Wilson Henszey,	Richard Peltz,
Samuel W. Cattell,	Robert W. Downing,	John L. Hill,	Wm. S. Stokley.

Secretary—FRANCIS DE HAES JANVIER.   Treasurer—PETER A. B. WIDENER.

Solicitor—CHARLES H. T. COLLIS.

Upon the conclusion of the Masonic ceremonies the orator of the day, Hon. BENJAMIN HARRIS BREWSTER, was introduced by Hon. WILLIAM S. STOKLEY, Mayor of the City.

Address

OF

HON. BENJAMIN HARRIS BREWSTER,

AT THE

LAYING OF THE CORNER STONE.

MR. PRESIDENT AND GENTLEMEN: These solemn ceremonies having been performed, it is now my duty to say some few words, explaining the history and purpose of this great public work. One hundred and eighty years ago, when this city and this province were a wilderness, William Penn, then the proprietor, dedicated this very spot of ground as the suitable site for the public buildings of his projected city. That such was his act, and such his purpose, has been judicially established as a legal and historic fact; and now we perform the conditions of the grant, and honestly apply the gift to the object of the trust, obeying the intentions of our provident benefactor.

For many years this city has been unprovided with buildings suitable for the convenient performance of the usual and necessary public business.

Before the consolidation of the city, as created by Penn, we were surrounded with outlying incorporated municipalities. Then the business of each and all was transacted with reasonable convenience in the old municipal buildings, and in the halls that had been erected in the districts and townships of the county; but even then the accommodations were wanting for the growing necessities of our courts. Year after year the officers of the county (then a separate and distinct corporation, with its own organization and officials) were driven to adopt expedients to supply the courts with convenient apartments. At one time the Supreme Court was held in the Hall of Independence; at another time the Supreme Court, Nisi Prius, was placed in the chapter room of the old abandoned Masonic Hall, Chestnut Street, above Seventh. During those days the necessities for such buildings for general public uses were few. Since then new and great departments have grown out of what were subordinate clerkships of public employment.

Day by day the want of proper apartments pressed upon the courts and interfered with the administration of justice. Day by day the same want crowded the officials of the city and the people who had business with them. There was hardly a county of any importance in the State that had not buildings larger in proportion to their wants, by a hundred fold, than our crowded and narrow rooms. Different plans had been projected and suggested for supplying this want. From many causes they all failed. Sometimes the fear of the cost hindered the prosecution of the purpose. Then the selection of the locality was in the way, and then the choice of the means by which it was to be done. At last the Legislature of the Commonwealth finally resolved, and by an Act, approved 5th of August, 1870, provided " for the erection of all of the public buildings required to accommodate the courts, and for all municipal purposes in the city of Philadelphia." That Act created the Commission now in charge of this duty, and gave the people of the city the privilege of indicating, by popular vote, whether the buildings should be at Washington Square or at Penn Square, where we now are, and where we have this day witnessed the laying of the corner stone of one of the most majestic and useful structures that adorn, or have adorned, any city of the world. MAY IT LAST FOR EVER!

After the passage of this Act a heated and almost angry opposition was excited; a series of litigations ensued; application was made to the Legislature; resistance was attempted in the City Councils, and the elements of the most vehement partisan prejudices were used to frustrate the law or secure its repeal. Then some of us regretted this opposition. Some thought it too personal, too violent. But since it has passed away all are reconciled, and believe that it was for the best. Such an event, conflicting as it did with so many convictions and interests, must excite opposition, and those who resisted had a right to be heard, and fully heard, before all of the tribunals, popular, legislative, and judicial. These contentions delayed the action of the Commission for any practical result for full a year. After that, all those obstructions being removed, it proceeded to act as the law commanded, as the people had directed, and as the courts had adjudged. What we now do is the product of that action. On the 7th of January, 1871, the work was first begun, by the removal of the iron railings which enclosed the four squares or plots of ground, into which the city had converted the whole, in the year 1828, for the purpose of running Market and Broad Streets through the original plot. Before that the place had been left as it was originally set apart—one entire square—and in that state had been occupied, at different times, and in different parts of it, by a Friends' meeting-house, and by the first water-works established and used for conveying Schuylkill water to the old city. I remember the small, neat building that graced the centre. I think it was designed by Latrobe, the famous architect, who adorned our city with some of its most beautiful structures, and who left the Capitol buildings at Washington as the highest achievement of his genius. The very columns that embellished its front now support the pediment of the Unitarian Church, at the corner of Tenth and Locust Streets. The bisection of this plot, by these highways, was for the purpose of temporary public convenience, and to accommodate the railways that were then for the first time introduced, and whose direct access to the city proper was considered to be of great importance to its trade and languishing commerce. With the growth of population and the changes of events that has passed away ; indeed the necessity now is to remove the railways from the thickly-peopled parts, where they are a dangerous obstruction to trade and the ordinary pursuits of the thousands who throng their crowded ways. It was at most but a temporary occupation and license, revocable at will, if it were not an unauthorized and illegal intrusion.

On the 10th of August, 1871, the ground was broken by John Rice, Esq., then President of the Board of Commissioners, and the first stone of the foundation was laid at 2 o'clock, P. M., on the 12th day of August, A. D. 1872. The closing of the streets and placing the building in the centre of the plot was the subject of much discussion in the Commission itself. By some it was wished that the streets should remain open, and the four plots should each contain a structure ; but the final resolution of the Commission was, and is, to place it and keep it where it was intended by Penn that it should be put—in the centre of the whole ten acres. And with this conclusion, I believe, most men now concur. It is the only place where a building of suitable dignity can stand to display its parts in all the beauty of their architectural effect. It will adorn, and not blemish, the highways at whose intersection it is placed, and it will give an air of majesty and grandeur to these long and broad avenues. It is not put in a corner, hidden from view, but it stands out in bold and high relief, commanding admiration. It is placed, as other and similar great structures are, as the centre of human concourse from which all things radiate and to which all things converge. It is surrounded by a grand avenue, 135 feet wide on the southern and eastern and western fronts, and 205 feet wide on the northern front. Neither the view nor way is hindered by it. The view is improved, the effect being magnified—and the way is widened into open spaces of unusual dimensions, but of proportions that harmonize with the magnitude of the building, and answer the convenience of the multitude that will be drawn here to transact public and private affairs. Had the buildings been divided and placed on the four squares, the cost would have been increased and their beauty lost, while the inconvenience to the public would have been great, and the expense of maintaining them with light and heat and water, and the other necessaries, would have been largely multiplied. The highways would have been smaller and narrower and less convenient. In this, as in all that has been done, these Commissioners have wisely followed, not forced, the general public judgment. Mr. John McArthur, Jr., of this city, who had before this been engaged in preparing all the previous plans, which had been the subject of public consideration for many years, was chosen the architect, and his plan adopted. That has been submitted to the public, and it, too, has been justly applauded and approved. I shall not here undertake to describe it by a multitude of words, which can only degenerate into mere rhetorical expletives, and would therefore be unsuitable as well as vulgar. This much, however, I must speak. It is suited for its purpose, it is of sufficient size to answer future wants. It is admirable in its ornaments, while the whole effect is one of massive dignity, worthy of us and our posterity.

I will here give the dimensions and a few of the details of this remarkable structure. It is 470 feet from east to west, and 486½ feet from north to south, covering an area, exclusive of the court-yard, of nearly four and a half acres. It is probably larger than any single building on this continent. The superstructure consists of a basement story, 18 feet in height, a principal story, of 36 feet, and an upper story, of 31 feet, surmounted by another of 15 feet. The small rooms opening upon the court-yard are each subdivided in height into two stories, for the purpose of making useful all the space. The several stories will be approached by four large elevators, placed at the intersections of the leading corridors, to make easy the intercourse of citizens with courts, public offices, and departments of city government. In addition to these means of access there will be a grand staircase in each of the four corners of the building, and one in each of the centre pavilions on the north, south, west and east fronts. The entire structure will contain five hundred and twenty rooms, of suitable dimensions, and fitted with every possible convenience, including heat, light, and ventilation, and the whole is to be absolutely fireproof and indestructible. All of the departments now existing will be abundantly supplied, and a vast amount of surplus room will be left for judicial and other city archives, as well as afford room for all of our growing wants. This is as it ought

KEY

SPANDRELS IN NORTHERN ENTRANCE.

to be. We provide for the present urgent wants, and protect the people hereafter from those inconveniences under which we now suffer, and which expose our records to ruin and decay, while they seriously obstruct and hurt all branches of business and public duty. It is computed that the entire cost of this work will be near ten millions of dollars, and that it will be completed in ten years from the day when the first spadeful of earth was removed.

To judge of its massive size, I will give you an account of what materials have been consumed in constructing the foundation and the parts of the superstructure you now see before you : 74,000 cubic feet of cement concrete, 636,400 cubic feet of foundation stone, 8,000,000 bricks, 70,000 cubic feet of dressed granite, and 366 tons of iron, including floor beams.

The excavation for the cellars and foundations required the removal of 141,500 cubic yards of earth. A large quantity of the marble for the superstructure has been prepared, and the corner stone is the first block that has yet been set in the building. Here I will end my details. To be more minute would be tedious and prolix ; but this much should be given to properly advise the public.

Let me state with accuracy to what purposes the building will be devoted, and who will occupy it the day it is ready for public use, that you may see and know what are our wants.

The Mayor will requre for the use of his office and of the police at least twelve commodious rooms.

The City Council Chambers and their officers will need	15
The City Treasurer,	3
The City Controller,	5
Law Department,	9
Water Department,	7
Highways, Bridges, and Sewers,	4
Survey Department,	4
Markets and City Property,	2
Building Inspectors,	2
Boiler Inspectors,	2
Health Office,	6
Fire Department,	4
Receiver of Taxes,	5
Police and Fire-alarm Telegraph,	2
Guardians of the Poor,	3
Port Wardens,	2
City Commissioners,	6
Coroner,	4
Girard Estates,	2

Board of Education,	6
Gas Office, ...	1
Park Commissioners, ...	1
Board of Revision, ...	4
Collector of Delinquent Taxes, ...	3
Courts, 13 rooms, with accommodations for the Prothonotaries and Clerks, for the Law Library, witness and jury rooms, and District Attorney.	
Recorder of Deeds,	4
Register of Wills,	4
Sheriff, . .	4

At this time the city rents apartments for the Recorder of Deeds, in the Philadelphia National Bank ; for the City Controller and Treasurer, in the Girard Bank ; the Law Buildings on Fifth Street, for the Law Department ; of the American Philosophical Society, for the Water Department ; and for the Survey Department, in No. 224 South Fifth Street ; in No. 723 Arch Street, for the Tax Office and Board of Revision ; and the southwest corner of Fifth and Walnut Streets, for the Department of Markets and City Property ; and for these insecure and unsuited places it pays a rent of $41,300. These I mention that it may be known and seen how scattered, costly, and unfit are our present accommodations for public purposes.

It will now be proper for me to speak a few words of the extent of our City of Homes, as it has been called, of its large accommodations for its people, of its great public improvements for public necessities and private comfort. This I will do in a cursory way, as the occasion and the time will not admit of precision and detail ; but it should be done, to show how fit this structure in all its magnitude of dimensions is for the community it is intended to supply, and how it harmonizes in all things with that which we have around us and about us in daily use, and how essential it is to construct it as it is designed, if we are to have a provident regard for the manifest wants of the future. I have seen and lived in almost all of the capitals of Europe, and I have read of all of the great cities of the world, but I have never seen or read of such a city as this is. There is no town in the world, of its dimensions or population, and there never has been one, that possesses such accommodations for its people.

Artisans, and even laborers, live with us as they never lived before. Men whose daily earnings in other cities will hardly sustain life and provide a shelter for themselves and their families, except in the most rude, coarse, scanty, and crowded way, are here the occupants of single and

CARYATIDES OF DORMER OF CORNE PAVILIANA

comfortable dwellings, and thousands of them the owners of their own
houses.

The effect of this upon the mental and moral condition of the citizens
is evident, even to transient visitors. We have no such class here as
the poor workingman ; our city is filled with workmen, independent,
prosperous freemen, who bring up families of boys with habits of thrift
and industry, to go out into life prepared and resolved to earn homes,
because they have enjoyed them in their happy childhood, and with good
girls, who are certain of provision for life with a comfortable house for
their families, because they are trained to keep those homes with tidiness
and economy, and because they are raised with a race of men who honor
and love their families, and find their only sense of content in the culti-
vation of the domestic affections. This is true, every word of it true,
of Philadelphia and its workmen. At the beginning of the year 1873
we had 134,740 buildings of all kinds. Of these 124,302 were dwell-
ing-houses, occupied by families. They exceed the following cities by
the following numbers :

New York, by over	60,000
Brooklyn, by over	78,000
St. Louis, by over	84,000
Baltimore, by over	83,000
Chicago, by over	79,000
Boston, by over .	94,000
Cincinnati, by over	99,000

This city has a population of near 800,000, and they live in an area
of 129⅛ square miles. It has 1000 miles of streets and roads opened
for use, and over 500 miles of these are paved. It is lighted by near ten
thousand gas lamps. The earth beneath conceals and is penetrated by
134 miles of sewers, over 600 miles of gas mains and 546 miles of water
pipes. We have over 212 miles of city railways, and near 1794 city
railroad cars passing over these railroads daily, 3025 steam boilers, over
400 public schools, with suitable buildings, and over 1600 school
teachers, and over 80,000 pupils. We have over 34,000 bath-rooms,
most of which are supplied with hot water, and for the use of the water,
at low rates, our citizens pay more than a million of dollars annually.
We have over 400 places of public worship, and accommodations in
them for 300,000 persons.

We have near 9000 manufactories, having a capital of $185,000,000,
employing 145,000 hands, the annual product of whose labor is over
$384,000,000. We exported in 1873, in value, over $34,000,000, and
we imported in value over $26,000,000. The amount paid for duties

in gold was near eight millions and a half. The real estate, as assessed for taxation, was over $518,000,000, and we collected near $9,000,000 for taxes. Our funded debt, including the gas loan, in January, 1873, was $51,697,147 67, and our annual outlay in 1873, inclusive of interest on our debt, was $7,726,123. We have parks and public squares, and Fairmount Park, which is one of them, contains 2991 acres, and is one of the largest parks in the world, and was enjoyed in 1873 by near 3,000,000 of people.

From this we can understand for whom we are now building, and why the outlay proposed is provident and necessary. We can also see in a partial way where our money has gone, but we can see with sufficient fullness how providently and judiciously most of it has been expended, when we behold this list of stupendous improvements, millions of which lie beneath the surface of the earth, and millions of which we drive over and walk over, unheeding the cost of the conveniences and comforts we are daily using in the paved, curbed, watered, drained, and lighted highways, on which front, for over 2000 miles, 124,302 neat and comfortable homes. I said, we can see in a partial way where our money has gone, because near twelve millions of the debt was incurred for the expenses of the civil war. But even that we can see and value, when, as the fruit of it, we can behold around us not only our own comfortable and peaceful homes, but we feel by its outlay, made with generous prodigality in such a cause, that we have saved a country and a free home for ourselves and for others in this land, and in foreign lands; and we feel that we have also shown that a republic can "maintain a perfect union, establish justice, insure domestic tranquillity, provide for the common defence, promote the general welfare, and secure the blessings of liberty for themselves and their posterity."

Of all the cities in this nation, Philadelphia is pre-eminently American. Philadelphia's characteristics and customs, the habits and peculiarities of the people, are essentially American. The vast body of its population is chiefly the product of its own people, who were here almost from the beginning. The descendants of the men who were here at its foundation, and were here at the outbreak of the Revolution, are the men who now compose the body of its citizens, who do its work, carry on its trades, make its ordinances, control its offices, own its property, and fill the stations of public usefulness and dignity. We are not governed by strangers, and have never been willing to submit to such rule. We have a manly local pride of citizenship; other seaboard cities are provincial, or filled with strangers from other parts of the nation and from other countries; and the Western cities are, like New York, the homes of new men from old places.

If a foreigner were to ask me, where will I find a real American, untouched in his character and nationality by the ever-drifting tide of emigration, domestic and foreign, and with no taint of provincial narrowness, I would say, go to Philadelphia, and there you will find just such men and women by the hundreds of thousands. There you will find a provident, steadfast race, the sons for over six generations of provident, steadfast ancestors; real Americans, bone of their bone, flesh of their flesh. Early in our career we commanded the foreign and domestic commerce of the colonies, and till 1820 this city was the commercial metropolis of the country. For a time that ascendency passed away, and New York, by her internal improvements, acquired the trade we had lost. While we thus ruled, we ruled grandly, and we have never forgotten our dignity. The sentiment that then prevailed with our people still prevails. Then they embellished our city with works of architecture, equalled nowhere in the Union in beauty and fitness. We then possessed nearly all of the public buildings and public works of the land, and they were objects of admiration. Strangers came from a distance to see them and enjoy them. The Fairmount Water Works, the old Bank of Pennsylvania, the old Bank of the United States (now the Girard Bank, both the works of Latrobe), the new Bank of the United States (now the Custom House), and the Exchange and the Mint of the United States, and the Naval Asylum (the works of Strickland), the old Philadelphia Bank, and such like, were scattered over our city, then small in its dimensions and population. Even in the earlier days we were not unmindful of what was due to good taste in the erection of our public structures, as well as in our beautiful private mansions that then stood surrounded with groves of trees adorning the town and country homes of our cultivated and wealthy colonial gentry and merchants. Let any one but step into Christ's Church, even as it is now changed by the renovating hand of modern improvement, and he will there see the remains of a harmony, simplicity, and fitness of adornment that indicates a high standard of just taste. And there is also the State House, in Chestnut Street. Enter the great hall that leads to the Hall of Independence and the tower, on which is built the steeple, and there will be seen a passage of modest dignity, and a broad, well-constructed stairway, showing that even in those days, over one hundred and twenty years ago, when it was built, surrounded with the forest trees, and out of town—in those simple days our ancestors had provided, as we provide, for the future and for public purposes, with a liberal hand, regarding taste as well as utility. Let us not forget the Pennsylvania Hospital in Pine Street, with its spacious grounds and its lofty, stately main building, at this day an object of admiration for its size and its proportions, so suited for its purpose, and so simple in its quiet, harmonious beauty.

All this we still have; and, further, we have the Girard College, with other grand and elegant structures that are the work of our own days. I will not speak of them in detail; time will not permit me to describe the rows of new residences that adorn our streets, or the costly and stately churches that are scattered in every quarter of the town. You have the great Masonic Temple and three beautiful churches that cluster round this very spot. I can remember well when but two steeples rose above our town; now, as you gaze from the summits in the Park, the city lies before you with a number of lofty domes and sky-piercing spires. These are the work of private enterprise and bounty. We must not omit to remember the great gift the city has this day bestowed upon her people. To-day the Girard Avenue Bridge was delivered over to the authorities, and is now possessed by all of us. It is a work of wonderful merit, and is well worth the millions spent on it. It is an avenue worthy of any of the greatest cities of the world. It contributes to our convenience and prosperity, while it bears witness to our pride and liberality of feeling in all that concerns the common and public good. In our growth we live up to the example of our ancestors, and have resolved now that for our present necessities, and according to the abundance of our means, we will adorn our city as it was adorned of old, with a structure that will fully answer its end, and command the admiration of all men.

Such is my love for and faith in this city, that I feel possessed with a conviction, which might even be called a superstition, that it will again be, as it once was, the real metropolis of the nation. The capital and the public offices of the Union will never return; the foreign trade may cluster at New York as it does in Liverpool; but Philadelphia will be again, as she first was, the real centre of finance, of commerce, and wealth. She is at the head of the mechanic arts and of manufacturing, and she has ever led in refinement, in science, and in jurisprudence. The material supremacies which left her will return, and those graces and glories which she has ever had will never leave her. Here they made their home, where Penn, the greatest of all the founders of free commonwealths, demonstrated that liberty, the largest liberty, was compatible with obedience to law, and a colony, established to maintain the firmest of religious convictions by the strictest of sects, could protect all other beliefs.

This wisdom he transmitted to our people, and as a body they possess it to this hour as a spirit or living public soul, and it is that which has made us just what we are, and for which we are and have been conspicuous in all of our public history. In the Revolution, when we had most to lose, we were first in action, and faithful to the end, enduring all things, hoping all things, believing all things for the love of that Christian liberty which was a part of our blessed faith. In those sad days, here came, as to a common centre, all of the wise and brave who guided and led in that contest. Here the Continental Congress sat, here the Declaration of Independence was written, executed and proclaimed. After the Revolution, here George Washington presided over the deliberation of the Constitutional Convention ; and here, too, he administered to the end of his official life the Government he had helped to form for the country he had saved. How thickly the memories of these events, our great events of the past, press on me! How the names of the wise and good and mighty rise up before me, and tempt me to enlarge upon the history of the grand things done, and of the men who did them. I mean those who belonged to us, who were Philadelphians, but whose fame is so large that men remember them only as belonging to mankind. We have had Penn and Franklin and Rittenhouse and Rush and Godfrey and Bartram, whose names posterity will not willingly let die. Penn and Franklin are names that never will be forgotten; they will pass down through time linked with Solon and Lycurgus, Pythagoras and Archimedes and Socrates and Plato and Aristotle, the crowned monarchs of human thought. But I must here pause. I have well-nigh done all that was required of me. I must not wander off, tempted by these proud thoughts of our proud citizenship. I never approach a great building but with a sense of awe. Mechanically I lift my hat, as if I stood in the august presence of something grand and good. I can understand why men have imputed spiritual gifts to the masters of this the greatest of all arts.

For in it all science and all art unite to produce sublime and almost supernatural results. Solomon, the wisest of men, thus illustrated the highest reaches of his superhuman genius, and the greatest achievement of the chosen people was the vast temple built by that monarch and dedicated to the service of Jehovah. Go where you will on the face of the earth, you will there find these grand works of nations now dead and perished from the memory of men. Those who made them had immortal souls ; but for this life they were mortal, and are no more remembered of men ; and yet thus their history is recorded and remembered in monuments that were the works of their minds and hands—

monuments that stand like great books written in the very rocks they are built upon. Where no such monuments are to be found the people had no mental or moral natures above the faculties of brutes. Wherever a nation had a conscience and a mind, there it recorded the evidence of its being in these the highest products of human thought, human knowledge, and human will.

It has been well said that architecture rests on two ideas—the natural, or the idea of order; the supernatural, or that of the infinite. In these various monuments of bygone ages these thoughts are displayed according to the genius of the people.

"In Greek art order directs and guides the natural and rational idea. The strong column elegantly grouped, bearing at its ease a light pediment—the weak rests on the strong; this is logical and human. Gothic art is supernatural—superhuman—it is born of the belief of the miraculous and poetic. The geometry of beauty bursts brilliantly forth in the type of the Gothic architecture in the Cathedral of Cologne. To whom belonged the science of numbers, this divine mathematics? To no mortal man did it belong, but to the Church of God. Under the shadow of the Church in chapters and in monasteries, the secret was transmitted, together with instructions in the mysteries of Christianity. The Church alone could accomplish these miracles of architecture. She could often summon a whole people to complete a monument. A hundred thousand men labored at once on that of Strasbourg, and such was their zeal that they did not suffer night to interrupt their work, but continued it by torchlight. Often, too, the Church would lavish centuries on the slow accomplishment of a perfect work."

The original and brilliant historian and thinker, whose words I have just repeated, citing them as the evidence of an observer, philosopher, and critic, conveys to us, in his clever sentences, those truths which illustrate and account for some of the most marvellous products of this mighty art. He reminds us that when pious zeal inspires, it passes beyond the mere love of order and fitness, and soars into the very empyrean of the miraculous and poetic. What a grand thing is it thus to perpetuate such sublimities of thought and feeling in monuments as everlasting as the hills, and as spiritual in their influence on the human soul! This is what we are doing. We are erecting a structure that will in ages to come speak for us as with "the tongues of men and angels." This work which we now do, as it were, in the morning hour of our being, will, probably, like the broken arch of London bridge fancied by Lord Macaulay, in some far off future day be all that remains to tell the story of our civilization, and to testify to the dignity and public spirit of our people.

EXTERIOR SPANDRELS AND KEY STONE OF NORTHERN ENTRANCE.

Photodyc

F. Gutekunst

Philadelphia.

What we thus give we must give with free spirit, not grudgingly, for as we are of great and good beginnings, and have been an earnest and noble race of men, so should we make this our monument tell the world and posterity how provident we are ; how, scorning ugliness as we do vice, we resolve thus to speak to men as it were in words of marble, that in their order are logical and human, and in their form reach to the miraculous and poetic.

We have done and are doing a great, great work, and it will inspire our posterity to live up to our standard, as we are inspired to live by the standard of our ancestors. They loved their town with a gentle fondness that is testified by every act of their useful and remarkable public lives, and they transmitted to us, their sons, the same soft sense of affection. We, too, can say, as Franklin said when writing of his home—dear, dear Philadelphia. Do we not say it in enduring words with this day's work, and when we leave behind us this noble building to say it for us ?

ONE OF EIGHT MEDALLIONS IN CONVERSATION HALL OF COUNCILS.

Philadelphia

Printed

SUMMARY

OF LEGISLATIVE AND MUNICIPAL ACTION RELATING TO THE WORK, WITH A BRIEF HISTORY OF EVENTS PERTAINING THERETO.

The earliest movements relating to the present undertaking consisted in the passage of an ordinance by the City Councils, approved December 31, 1868, providing for the erection of Municipal Buildings on Independence Square, and designating Commissioners to carry the same into effect.

The first meeting of the Commission was held in the Select Council Chamber, January 7, 1869.

Architectural designs were advertised for on the 5th of April, 1869, and on the 1st of September following, plans and drawings had been received from seventeen different architects.

At a meeting of the Commissioners, held September 27, 1869, the first premium was awarded to John McArthur, Jr., architect, of this city, and on the 27th of the following December, Mr. McArthur was appointed Architect of the work, and proposals for labor and materials were ordered to be advertised for.

Contracts were awarded on the 16th of January, 1870, and arrangements made for commencing the work.

A strong opposition to Independence Square, as the site for the Municipal Buildings, had existed in the public mind from the earliest movements in that direction, and as the Commission proceeded with their preparations for carrying out the provisions of the ordinance under which they were acting, the opposition became daily more intensified, until it culminated in the passage of a law by the Legislature of the State, approved August 5, 1870, providing for the erection of the Public Buildings either on Washington Square or on Penn Square, as the legally qualified voters of the City of Philadelphia might determine, at the general election to be held in October, 1870. The election resulted, out of a total of 84,450 votes, in a majority of above 18,800 in favor of the site on Penn Square, which finally disposed of the question. The passage of this law rendered the municipal ordinance of no effect, and relieved the Commissioners acting under it of further duties.

The first meeting of the Commissioners, under the new law, was held on the 27th of August, 1870, at the Mayor's Office.

There were present Hon. Daniel M. Fox, Mayor of the City; Samuel W. Cattell, President of Select Council; Louis Wagner, President of Common Council; with all the Commissioners designated by name in the Act, except William Devine, deceased, and William L. Stokes, not known; and Messrs. Henry W. Gray and William S. Stokley were elected in their places. A temporary organization was effected by the election of Mayor Fox as President, and Eugene G. Woodward, Secretary.

September 15, 1870, John McArthur, Jr., was elected Architect of the work.

October 4, 1870, a permanent organization was made, and John Rice was elected President, Charles R. Roberts, Secretary, and Charles H. T. Collis, Solicitor.

November 1, 1870, the Commissioners decided to have one building, and to locate it on the intersection of Broad and Market Streets, and on the third day of the same month proposals for labor and materials were advertised for.

The removal of the iron railings which enclosed the four squares on Broad and Market Streets was commenced on the 27th of January, 1871, and this may properly be considered as the date of the actual beginning of the work.

At a meeting of the Commissioners, held June 19, 1871, a resolution was passed to the effect, " That any and all action heretofore had by the Board, designating the intersection of Market and Broad Streets as the site for the Public Buildings, is hereby repealed, annulled, and made void ;" and the Architect was directed to prepare plans for the buildings on the four squares, fronting on Market and Broad Streets.

The Architect submitted to the Board, August 7, 1871, designs for the four separate buildings, as directed, whereupon the same were adopted ; and on the 16th of the same month the ground was formally broken by John Rice, Esq., then President of the Commission.

Impediments were from time to time interposed to the progress of the work, by application to the Courts, on various grounds, for injunctions, to which is to be attributed the delay which attended the early stages of the enterprise.

October 12, 1871, Francis De Haes Janvier was elected Secretary, in place of Mr. Roberts, resigned, and John Sunderland was elected Superintendent.

At a meeting of the Commissioners, held April 7, 1872, it was re-solved to revert to the original idea of placing the buildings on the intersection of Market and Broad Streets. The architectural plans and drawings having been heretofore prepared for the work under the original instructions of the Commissioners, and the excavations answer-ing in part for either location, the change from the four buildings to the intersection involved no delay. The first stone was laid on the 12th of August, 1872.

On the 17th of April, 1872, Mr. Rice resigned as President of the Commissioners, and Samuel C. Perkins was elected in his place.

The contract for the granite basement was awarded November 19, 1872, for $515,500; and work was commenced under the contract, March 24, 1873. The contract for the marble work of the super-structure was awarded on the 7th of October, 1873, for $5,300,000 ; the form of the contract in all its details was approved and adopted, November 26, 1873, and ordered to be executed by the President on behalf of the Commissioners ; it was actually executed December 18, 1873, and as executed submitted to the Commissioners at their stated meeting, January 6, 1874, and then formally ratified. The first block under this contract was set in the walls, July 3, 1874.

November 4, 1873, William C. McPherson was elected Superintendent, and entered upon his duties November 10.

The appropriations by Councils for the prosecution of the work, up to 1879, inclusive, have been as follows:—

1872, April 6, 1872 (Ord. p. 120),
    Items 1 to 9 for 1870, 1871, . $18,700 00
    Items for 1872,   .   .   258,750 00
    ————— $277,450 00
1872, Dec. 28 (Ord. p. 641), for 1873, .   769,750 00
1873, May 12 (Ord. p. 201), for 1873
    (proceeds Water Pipe),   1,209 88
    ————— 770,959 88
1873, Dec. 20 (Ord. p. 618), for 1874, . . . 1,457,450 00
1874, Oct. 26 (Ord. p. 314), warrants to amount of $500,000 of the $1,457,450 to be approved and paid from amount of general tax and provided for out of special tax of 1875.
1874, Dec. 28 (Ord. p. 452), for 1875,   875,750 00
1875, Dec. 31 (Ord. p. 434), for 1876,   . . 595,000 00
1876, May 13 (Ord. p. 108), warrants to amount of $500,000 of the appropriation to be paid out of general tax.
No appropriation for 1877.
1878, March 23 (Ord. p. 56), for 1878,   600,000 00
1879, January 4 (Ord. p. 2), for 1879,   . 750,000 00
    ————— $5,326,609 88

Of this amount there had been collected by special tax, up to December 31, 1879, inclusive, $3,333,270.

The year 1876 was the last for which a special tax was levied for the Public Buildings. The amounts collected in subsequent years were arrears from former years.

Councils, by Ordinance of December 31, 1879, appropriated for the prosecution of the work in 1880, $635,000.

Expenditures out of APPROPRIATIONS by Councils:—

1872.	Expended,	$156,026	17
1873.	"	438,241	45
1874.	"	1,007,725	89
1875.	"	1,401,425	23
1876.	"	758,683	15
1877.	"	146,192	98
1878.	"	643,162	72
1879.	"	745,315	13

$5,296,772 72

Less warrant returned and cancelled,   187 52
           $5,296,585 20

Amount of special warrants paid to William Struthers & Sons, and collected by mandamus under the decision of the court, ... $265,196 26

Amount of special warrants paid to William Struthers & Sons, up to December 31, 1879, inclusive, and remaining uncollected at that date, .   . 295,836 88
           $561,033 14

Total amount expended to Dec. 31, 1879, inclusive, $5,857,618 34

SINCE THE FIRST MEETING OF THE COMMISSIONERS
THE FOLLOWING CHANGES HAVE TAKEN PLACE
IN THE MEMBERSHIP OF THE BODY.

1871. Jan'y 2. Henry Huhn, *ex officio* as President of Common
Council, in place of Louis Wagner.

Oct. 19. Theodore Cuyler and Henry M. Phillips, resigned.

Nov. 15. William Massey and Mahlon H. Dickinson, elected
in place of Messrs. Cuyler and Phillips.

1872. Jan'y 1. William S. Stokley, *ex officio* as Mayor, in place of
Daniel M. Fox.

William E. Littleton, *ex officio* as President of Select
Council, in place of Samuel W. Cattell.

Jan'y 2. John Price Wetherill and William Massey, resigned.

Jan'y 18. John L. Hill and R. J. C. Walker, elected in place
of Messrs. Wetherill and Massey.

William S. Stokley resigned his individual membership. Henry W. Gray, resigned.

Samuel W. Cattell and Alexander M. Fox, elected
in place of Messrs. Stokley (individually) and
Gray.

Feb'y 13. Alexander M. Fox declined his election, and Hiram
Miller elected in his place.

Feb'y 15. Louis Wagner, *ex officio* as President of Common
Council, in place of Henry Huhn, who had resigned the office.

April 17. William Brice and Thomas J. Barger, elected to fill
up the number of Commissioners to thirteen.

May 14. R. J. C. Walker resigned.

May 28. John Rice resigned, and Richard Peltz elected.

July 12. Thomas E. Gaskill elected in place of Mr. Walker.

SPANDRELS AND KEY STONE OF CORNER PAVILION.

Philadelphia.

P. Gutekunst

Photdtype.

1873. Jan'y 6. A. Wilson Henszey, *ex officio* as President of Common Council, in place of Louis Wagner.

1874. Jan'y 5. Robert W. Downing, *ex officio* as President of Select Council, in place of William E. Littleton.

1875. July 8. William W. Burnell, M.D , *ex officio* as President of Select Council, in place of Robert W. Downing.

1876. Jan'y 3. George A. Smith, *ex officio* as President of Select Council, in place of William W. Burnell, M.D.

Joseph L. Caven, *ex officio* as President of Common Council, in place of A. Wilson Henszey.

1877. June 12. Lewis C. Cassidy resigned.

Dec. 4. Isaac S. Cassin elected in place of Mr. Cassidy.

PLACES OF MEETING OF COMMISSIONERS.

The earlier meetings were held at the office of the Mayor. From October, 1870, the Commissioners met in one of the lower rooms of the new Court House on Independence Square, until September, 1871, with the exception of a few meetings held at the Architect's office, to examine plans, &c. In September, 1871, rooms were rented for the use of the Commissioners in the second story of No. 1107 Chestnut Street, and occupied for a month, when the Commissioners removed to rooms in the second story of No. 1103 Chestnut Street. In November, 1872, the premises No. 1408 S. Penn Square, and opposite the site of the Buildings, were rented and used as the offices and place of meeting of the Commissioners, until November, 1875, when rooms were fitted up for their accommodation in the basement on the southern side of the Buildings themselves ; the first meeting therein was held November 2, 1875.

DESCRIPTION OF THE BUILDINGS.

THE EXTERIOR.

A tendency exists in the public mind to seek to classify every considerable architectural design under the head of some "order" or "style;" but modern genius and taste deal so largely in original adaptations of classic and other forms that we often find no small difficulty in deciding under which, if any, of the heretofore established *orders* or *styles* many of the most important structures of the present day can properly be classed.

The architecture of the New Public Buildings is of this character. It is essentially modern in its leading features, and presents a rich example of what is known by the generic term of the "Renaissance," modified and adapted to the varied and extensive requirements of a great American municipality.

It is designed in the spirit of French art, while at the same time its adaptation of that florid and tasteful manner of building is free from servile imitation, either in ornamentation or in the ordonnance of its details.

This immense architectural pile is located on the intersection of Broad and Market Streets, in the City of Philadelphia. It consists of a single building, under one roof, occupying, inclusive of the court-yard, an area of nearly 4½ acres. The horizontal dimensions of the structure are a square of 425 feet, with added projections for convenience and architectural effect, making its extreme length 470 feet from east to west, and 486½ feet from north to south.

The four fronts are similar in design. In the centre of each an entrance pavilion, of 86 feet in width, rises to the height of 201 feet, flanked by receding wings of 53 feet in length by 130 feet elevation, and receding curtains 118 feet high and 68½ feet long, terminating at

ORNAMENTS IN WINDOW JAMBS.—CORNER PAVILION.

Photype

F. Gutekunst

Philadelphia

each of the four corners of the building with towers or pavilions of 48 feet square, and 161 feet high.

The whole exterior is bold and effective in outline, and rich in detail, being elaborated with highly ornate columns, pilasters, pediments, cornices, enriched windows, and other appropriate adornments, wrought in artistic forms, expressing American ideas and developing American genius.

The main entrances open through the centre pavilions on the four fronts, affording passages for pedestrians up and down Broad and Market Streets, directly through the basement story. Each of these entrances is 18 feet wide and 36 feet high, finished with ornamented archivolts and richly sculptured spandrels.

The basement story is 18 feet high, and stands entirely above the line of the pavement. Its exterior is composed of fine white granite of massive proportions, forming a fitting base for the vast superstructure it supports.

The exterior of the building, above the basement, includes a principal story of 36 feet, and an upper story of 31 feet; the centre pavilions having each an additional story of 27 feet, surmounted by an attic of 15 feet, crowned with a massive dormer window in marble, of 42 feet in height, flanked by marble caryatides 20 feet 9 inches high. The corner pavilions are each surmounted by an attic of 12 feet in height.

The entire superstructure, including all its mural embellishments, is composed of white marble from the quarries at Lee, in Berkshire county, Massachusetts.

A court-yard of 186 feet north and south by 220 feet east and west is located in the centre of the structure, which, together with two additional open areas, each measuring 45 feet north and south by 69 feet east and west, afford abundance of light and air to all the adjacent portions of the building. The principal stories facing the court-yard are, for the most part, each divided by a mezzanine or half story, affording increased space for smaller rooms.

From the north side of the central court-yard rises a grand tower of

90 feet square at the base, gracefully falling off at each story until it becomes, at the spring of the dome (which is 315 feet above the level of the court-yard), an octagon of 56 feet in diameter, tapering to the height of 84 feet, where it is crowned with a statue of the founder of Pennsylvania, 36 feet in height, thus completing the extraordinary altitude of 535 feet, making it the highest artificial construction in the world, while at the same time it possesses the elements of firmness and stability equal in degree to those of any known structure of like character.

The foundations of this tower are laid on a bed of solid concrete, eight feet thick, at the depth of 20 feet below the surface of the ground, and its walls, which at the base are 22 feet in thickness, are built of dressed dimension stones, weighing from two to five tons each.

THE INTERIOR.

The entire structure will contain 520 rooms, affording ample, convenient, and stately accommodations for the immediate wants of all the Departments of the City Government included under the heads of Legislative, Executive, and Judicial; besides which, an amount of surplus room remains for use in the classification and preservation of the archives of the city, for storage and for increased accommodations, which will undoubtedly be required from time to time by the natural increase of the public business and the accumulation of the public records.

The actual floor room included within the walls amounts to 631,438 superficial feet, or 14½ acres, inclusive of the sub-basement, which extends under the whole structure.

The several stories will be approached by four large *elevators*, located at the intersections of the leading corridors, so as to facilitate the intercourse of the citizens with the public offices, courts, and other branches of the Government. In addition to these means of approach there will be large and convenient stairways in the four corner buildings, and a grand staircase in each of the centre pavilions, on the north, south, and east fronts.

Every room in the building will be well lighted, warmed, and ventilated, upon a thorough, effective, and approved system, and every part of the structure will be absolutely fireproof.

The heating and ventilating apparatus for the eastern half of the work is now virtually completed, and in operation. The system adopted to accomplish these objects consists in drawing a given quantity of pure external air from the court-yard into passages 15 feet wide and 11 feet high, constructed for the purpose, under all the corridors of the basement story, and forcing it, by means of a steam fan, among and around stacks of radiators heated by steam boilers, into all the rooms and corridors of the basement and superstructure of the eastern half of the building.

The fan is located in the southern portion of the sub-basement. It has a disc of 12 feet in diameter, with 16 wings on each side, and is capable of delivering 855 cubic feet of air per each revolution. It is driven by a horizontal engine of 20 horse power, and admits of being run up to 120 revolutions per minute, which will deliver throughout the eastern half of the building at the rate of 102,564 cubic feet of air per minute.

The warm air is generated by 6 half tubular boilers, 60 inches in diameter and 14 feet long, each containing 43 *four-inch* tubes, and a steam dome 30 inches in diameter and 30 inches high. The boilers are each 65¾ horse power, making an aggregate of horse power amounting to 394½. They are set in nests of *three*, and the pipes and connections are so arranged that each boiler may be used independently or in connection, as may be required.

This process of heating produces a forced ventilation, inasmuch as the air introduced into the rooms of necessity displaces an equal quantity of vitiated air, which escapes through ventilating registers opening near the floor in every room, and connecting with large exhaust shafts which discharge at the height of 170 feet above the level of the ground.

None of the apparatus for heating and ventilating the western half of the building is yet provided for.

The following materials have been used in the foundations and in the portions of the superstructure already executed, to wit:—

80,325 cubic feet of concrete foundations.

824,865 cubic feet of foundation stone from Conshohocken, Pa.

190,703 cubic feet of dressed granite, in the exterior of the basement and sub-basement, from Concord, N. H., and Blue Hill, Maine.

344,980 cubic feet of marble, actually set.

32,350 cubic feet of marble on the ground, ready to set.

8,625 cubic feet of marble at the shops, wrought and being wrought.

10,800 cubic feet of marble at the shops, in the rough.

———

396,755 cubic feet of marble in all, from Lee, Mass.

65,500 cubic feet of buff and blue sandstone, from Ohio.

12,800 cubic feet of polished granite, from the quarries on the Magaguadavic River, near St. George, N. B., and from Quincy and Cape Ann, Mass.

7,500 cubic feet of hammered granite, from Concord, N. H.

12,500 cubic feet of polished marble, from Pennsylvania and from Rutland, Vt.

40,185,950 hard bricks.

159,800 pressed bricks.

105,000 white bricks.

78,096 enameled bricks.

680 tons of wrought iron floor beams.

74 tons of wrought iron clamps, tie-rods, bolts, braces, compound girders, &c.

731 tons of cast iron ceilings, lintels, plates, askewbacks, iron bricks, cast iron door and window trimmings, &c.

23,750 square feet of bond slate.

The excavations for the cellars and the foundations required the removal of 145,870 cubic yards of earth.

SPANDRELS AND KEY STONE OF NORTHERN ENTRANCE.

Photatype.

F. Gutekunst.

Philadelphia.

The preparation of the ground for excavations involved the change of the gas pipes, and of the two water mains of 20 and 30 inches in diameter, from their course through the centre of Broad Street, to a circuit around the site of the buildings. The tracks of the West Philadelphia Passenger Railway were changed from the centre of Market Street and laid around the site ; and the Freight Railroad owned by the city, and which ran through Market Street, was entirely removed after it had ceased to be of use in the transportation of materials for the buildings. These changes involved a heavy outlay, which was charged to the Commissioners.

The entire ornamentation of the stone work of the exterior, and also the decorative work of the dressed stone for interior finish, has been carved in this city from models specially prepared by Alexander M. Calder and his assistant, James G. C. Hamilton. A large room in the basement on the western side of the southern entrance has been used as a modelling room since October, 1877.

The Supreme Court of the State has had its accommodations since January 1, 1877 (including the Prothonotary's Office), on the first story of the south front, occupying all the rooms on the south side of the corridor west of the centre pavilion. The addresses delivered at the opening of the session, Monday, January 1, 1877, are reported in Vol. 82 of Pennsylvania State Reports (1 Norris).

The Highway Department was opened for business in the New Buildings December 10, 1878, occupying rooms on the first story of the eastern front south of the central pavilion.

The Survey Department removed July 1, 1879, to rooms south of the central pavilion, on the same floor and front with the Highway Department.

The Head-Quarters of the Division, and of the First Brigade of the National Guard of Pennsylvania, were provided with convenient rooms adjoining those intended for the Department of Markets and City Property, and on November 1, 1879, Major-General John F. Hartranft and Brigadier-General George R. Snowden, commanding the Division and Brigade, took possession of their respective quarters.

Since January 1, 1880, the following Departments have removed to rooms fitted up for their accommodation in the new buildings:

Boiler Inspectors, January 17, 1880.
Board of Revision of Taxes, March 1, 1880.
Markets and City Property, April 21, 1880.
Receiver of Taxes, May 3, 1880.